Fungi lurk in the ground and in trees. They float on a breeze. You might find them in your refrigerator, or even in space.

By Darlyne A. Murawski

It's late at night. I turn off my flashlight. The forest is dark. Then, I see a strange light. There! It's coming from a patch of orange mushrooms. They glow in the dark.

Looking for mushrooms is like a treasure hunt for me. I'm a scientist. I **observe** living things. Some forms of life are really surprising. That's why I like mushrooms and other **fungi** (FUHN jye or FUHN gye). They may be the most surprising of all.

A Kingdom of Their Own

Fungi are not plants. Plants make their own food. Fungi can't do that. Fungi aren't animals, either. Animals can move on their own. Fungi can't. So what are they?

Fungi belong to a special **kingdom**, or group of living things. That group includes mushrooms, yeast, lichens, and mold.

As many as 1.5 million kinds of fungi grow on Earth. You can find them almost everywhere. Most grow in warm, moist places. Some can grow where it's really cold, though. Some even grow in the space station!

Night Lights. At night (top), these Jack-o'-lantern mushrooms glow in the dark.

4

NATIONAL GEOGRAPHIC

Fun Fungi

PIONEER EDITION

By Darlyne A. Murawski

CONTENTS

2   Fungus Among Us

10   Mushrooms, Molds, & More

12   Concept Check

Fungus Among Us

Lacy Veils. *Why do you think these mushrooms are called veiled ladies?*

Stranger Danger. *Many mushrooms are poisonous. Some that are safe to eat have poisonous look-alikes. So look, but don't touch or taste.*

Ruby Red. *These red mushrooms look like fancy hats.*

Blue Bell. *Fungi come in many colors. Here's a bright blue one.*

Hidden World

For most of its life, a mushroom lives underground. A new mushroom starts with a tiny **spore**. The spore grows. It sends out a thread.

The thread branches and spreads. It forms a thick mat. Threads from two spores may join. They can make a "fruitbody." That's a mushroom! It pushes out of the ground. It grows a stipe (or stalk) and a cap.

Thin plates called gills grow under the cap. They hold millions of spores.

The spores ripen and fall. They float away on the wind. Some travel for many miles. Then they drop to the ground. The life cycle of the mushroom continues.

Look Closely. *Many spores cover the gill of a mushroom.*

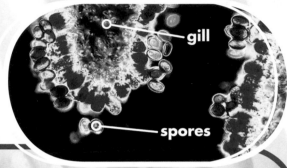

gill

spores

Meet a Mushroom

Gills hold the spores.

The **cap** is the top of the mushroom.

The **stipe** (or stalk) holds up the cap.

Spreading Spores

Some mushrooms spread spores in other ways. Some have strong smells that attract flies. Spores stick to a fly's feet. The fly carries the spores away.

One kind of fungus looks like a nest of eggs. The egg-shaped parts are full of spores. When it rains, the "eggs" splash to the ground. They break open and spores spill out.

My favorite fungus is called the hat-thrower. It has a small bubble below its cap. The sun warms the air in the bubble. The air gets hot and expands. The bubble explodes. *Pop!*

The cap flies into the air. So do the spores. Some stick to leaves. Animals eat the leaves. The spores pass through the animal. Perfect! New hat throwers can grow now.

Egg Imitator. *Each bird's nest fungus is about the size of a pea.*

Hat Trick. *Heat makes the bubble on this hat thrower pop. The black cap flies off.*

black cap

bubble

7

Soupy Goo

To grow, fungi need to eat. Unlike plants, they can't make their own food. They have to find food. Luckily, it's right where they grow!

Many grow on dead things, including animals. The fungi ooze a chemical. It turns the dead stuff into soupy goo. Then they absorb the goo.

That sounds gross. But it's a good thing. Fungi are a big part of the food chain. They are **decomposers**. They turn nature's trash into food. That helps clean up the forest, too.

A few fungi are predators. They set traps under the ground. They catch and eat worms. Yum!

Fungus Farmers

Of course, it's often the fungi that become the meal. Have you ever eaten a pizza with mushrooms? Then you've eaten fungi! The yeast in pizza dough is a fungus, too.

Deer, slugs, and fungus beetles also eat fungi. So do leaf-cutter ants. In fact, they are fungus farmers. They trim bits of leaves from plants. They carry the leaves to a fungus garden. The fungi eat the leaves and grow. Then the ants eat bits of fungi.

You don't have to go far to find fungi. I find plenty in my yard. You can, too. So go on a fungus hunt. You may be surprised at what you find.

Forest Cleaners. *Over time, mushrooms like these will eat this entire log. That helps clean up the forest.*

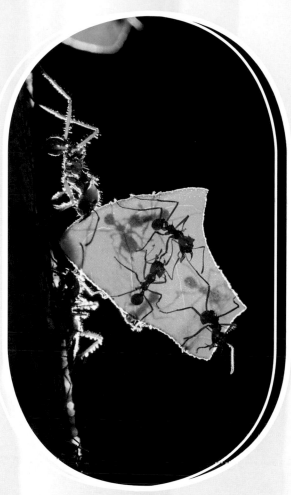

Fungus Food. *These leaf-cutter ants carry leaves to their fungus garden.*

Bright Beetle. *This fungus beetle stands on a mushroom like a shelf. It grows out of a tree trunk.*

Mushrooms, Molds, & More

As many as 1.5 million species of fungi grow on Earth. They include mushrooms, lichens, and molds. Check out these amazing fungi facts.

This black, fuzzy mold commonly grows on fruits and vegetables. Here's an up-close look.

During the day, these mushrooms look tan. At night, though, they glow in the dark.

Did you know some molds can be good for you? This one is! It's used to make the medicine penicillin.

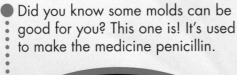

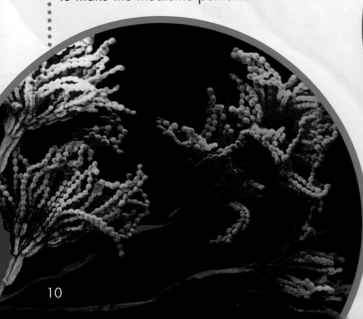

These fungi look like a stack of pancakes. They smell almost as sweet—like watermelon rind!

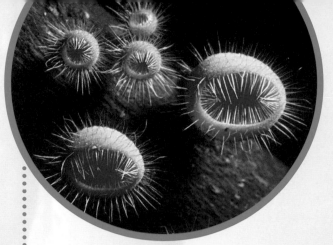

Are these aliens? The tiny orange fungi look just like something from outer space. They grow on wood in tropical areas.

smoke-like spores

The outer layer of this earthstar mushroom peels back into a star shape. Just a drop of rain releases its spores. They puff out like a cloud of smoke.

These lichens are flat and crinkly. They grow on almost any surface, including rocks.

red fruitbody

These are British soldier lichens. They are the same red color as a British soldier's uniform. Lichens are part fungi and part algae.

This may be a beautiful mushroom, but it stinks! The veiled lady is a stinkhorn mushroom. Its rotting-meat odor attracts flies.

Spores Galore

Now it is time to uncover the facts you learned about fungi.

1 Why are fungi not like plants or animals?

2 Explain three ways mushrooms spread their spores.

3 How do fungi get their food?

4 How would our world be different without decomposers?

5 What other kinds of fungi are there besides mushrooms? Which one interests you the most? Why?